Diversity Breakthroug

Achievement

Measuring Progress; Celebrating Success

Debbe Kennedy

Foreword by
Bert Bleke
Superintendent,
Lowell Area Schools

BK Berrett-Koehler **Communications**
San Francisco

Berrett-Koehler Communications, Inc.
450 Sansome Street, Suite 1200
San Francisco, CA 94111-3320

ORDERING INFORMATION:
Send orders to Berrett-Koehler Communications, Inc. P.O. Box 565, Williston, VT 05495-9900 or place your order by calling 800-929-2929, faxing 802-864-7626 or visiting www.bkconnection.com. Special discounts are available on quantity purchases. For details call toll free 800-929-2929. Ask for item number 60547.

Illustrations and layout by Sally K. Green

Printed in the United States of America

ISBN 1-58376-054-7

Table of Contents

Foreword
Bert Bleke, Superintendent, *Lowell Area Schools* 5

Introduction *Achievement—Measuring Progress; Celebrating Success* 7

Starting *Setting Direction; Defining Actions* 11
A five-step assessment and action planning process

What YOU Can Do Strategies
- Action planning worksheets to guide your thinking and decisions.
- Action-directed strategy ideas and suggestions to prompt your own thinking.
- Stories from other organizations to inspire your action.

Leadership *Reflecting on accomplishments* 17
The Human Will to Change - Debbe Kennedy - page 16

Culture *Celebrating diversity, inclusion & renewal* 23
Smiles Are Passports - Catherine DeVrye - page 22

Involvement *Recognizing contributions; fueling next steps* 29
Bringing People Together - IBM Corporation - page 28

The Business *Connecting the best in people with results achieved* 35
New Language for Success - Hewlett-Packard Company - page 34

Strategies & Measures *Focusing on accomplishments* 41
Achievement Without Numbers - U.S. Army - page 40

Staffing & Development *Acknowledging the changing human landscape* 47
The Power of Potential - Leap Wireless International - page 46

Ownership *Seeing how far we have come* 53
Learning to Trust - The Burgundy Group - page 52

A Call-to-Action *Truth in Numbers* 57

Contributing Organizations *Learning from Role Models* 58

Notes & Sources 60

About the Author 61

About the Diversity Breakthrough! Action Series 62

About Berrett-Koehler Communications 64

"I would like to be known as a person who is concerned about freedom and equality and justice and prosperity for all people."

—Rosa Parks
Recipient of the U.S. Presidential Medal of Freedom

Foreword

If your organization is measuring progress and achievements, I assume you have been working to create a better place for people for some time. So have we. Although we may come from different places and work in different kinds of organizations, if we could talk about our experiences in leading change—creating environments where character, diversity and inclusion are valued—we would find many similarities.

We are a relatively small school district located in a changing community just outside the metropolitan area of Grand Rapids, Michigan. A few years ago, the development of five character traits began to change our schools and our community: *Responsibility, Integrity, Compassion, Honesty* and *Respect.* Our first achievement was a gathering of over 300 students, parents, teachers, administrators and clergy that helped choose the traits we felt would be the most powerful influence on our kids, organization and community. We knew we could not change the culture of our school system—and certainly not an entire community—overnight. Our second achievement was deciding we would take the one, two or three years necessary to allow people the opportunity to question, wonder and decide for themselves what the words meant and how living these values would be important to them. Over time, administrators, the teachers, as well as others in the community, joined the effort. Last year, we formed a district-wide committee to put together specific action plans that will help us take other important steps. What we have learned is that if you slowly develop a culture about respect, character and caring for others, in a very quiet way, but a most powerful way, it begins to guide people's action—there is the big achievement.

If enough of us get involved, it can be better. That is the power of separate organizations—different perspectives and approaches. There is no one recipe for making a difference. We have to learn to measure our victories and progress by new standards. If we all just work on ourselves a little bit, it will be a better world. The idea is not to change the world. The idea is to try to change the block you are living on.

Bert Bleke
Superintendent
Lowell Area Schools

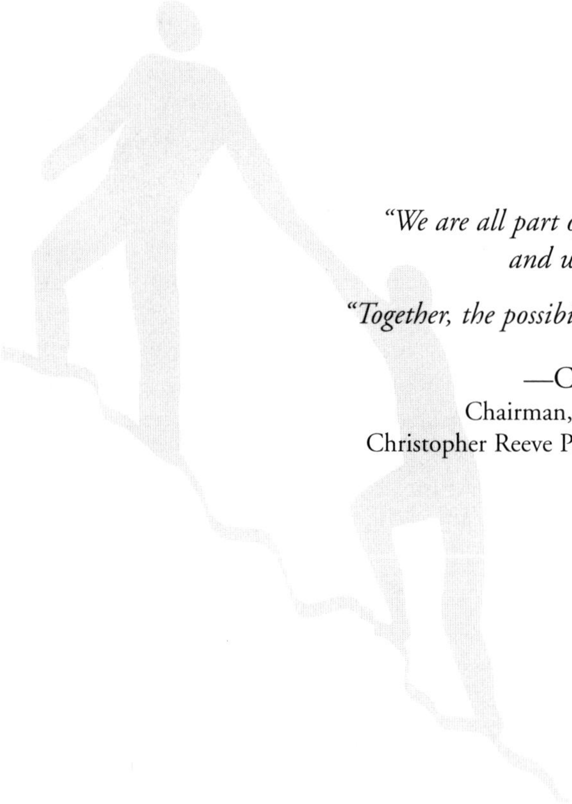

"We are all part of the same family
and we are all valued."

"Together, the possibilities are endless."

—Christopher Reeve
Chairman, Board of Directors
Christopher Reeve Paralysis Foundation

Introduction

Achievement—Measuring Progress; Celebrating Results

Diversity and inclusion carry with them a legacy of achievements marked by courageous leadership and sacrifice. We all have vivid memories of *the power of one* and *the power of many* opening the way. We seldom see our individual contributions as a part of that continuing legacy—our hard work and seemingly small successes, in the name of fundamental fairness, diversity and inclusion, pass by most of us with seldom more than a moment's notice. Whether we successfully complete a big event with great influence, see statistical reports showing organizational progress or recognize the difference in someone's life we may have touched, the achievements are fleeting—we only see there is so much left to do. Perhaps there isn't time to linger on our successes, but we can harness them. Acknowledge them. Revisit them over and over again to help us see how far we have come, encourage us to start again and give us the will to do more.

Some years back, by chance, I discovered the vital role *progress* and *achievement* play in reaching goals. The first Monday morning after I left IBM, I traced how dreams had come true for me in those *twenty-one* years. It says a lot about the value of measuring process and celebrating achievements —and their important roles in fueling our successes.

OUR DREAMS IN ACTION

> Dreams give us hope.
> Hope ignites passion.
> Passion leads us to envision success.
> Visions of success open our minds to recognize opportunity.
> Recognition of opportunities inspires far-reaching possibilities.
> Far-reaching possibilities help us enlist support from others.
> Support from others keeps us focused and committed.
> Focus and commitment foster action.
> Action results in progress.
> Progress leads to achievement.
> Achievement inspires dreams.
> Dreams give us hope.

When Dr. Martin Luther King, Jr. said *"I have a dream today,"* he stepped us through his *dream in action*—defining the measures of achievement. His success in reaching us decades later continues to inspire a great deal of hard work. Explore how your achievements can begin to do the same.

About This Book

This *Achievement: Measuring Progress; Celebrating Success* book is part of the *Diversity Breakthrough! Strategic Action Series.* It is designed to help you and your organization develop ways to monitor, measure and celebrate progress as you create a diverse, inclusive organization ready for the opportunities of the 21st Century. Whether you are launching a new initiative to create a diverse and inclusive organization or you are working to renew and revitalize an existing one, you will find helpful information, advice from others, inspiration and tools to create your own action plan for *measuring progress* and *celebrating success.* Included are:

- exercises to help you build a preliminary reference point, identify priorities based on current knowledge and develop an action plan,
- stories, advice and insights about what others have experienced,
- strategy ideas and suggestions to stimulate your thinking and action,
- historical and contemporary quotes and perspectives from great leaders, sages and thinkers to guide, validate actions and inspire you.

Discover Your Own Powerful Ideas

Although the insights, ideas and suggestions presented in this book can be implemented *as is,* the intent of offering them is to stimulate your own thinking and action. Over the years, I have confirmed over and over again that the leaders and people within an organization know best what to do for their organization. In the presence of a few good ideas, they do their best work. I liken this to how a long jump athlete takes a running start before actually jumping. Ideas create thinking momentum. Someone else's ideas work like springboards to help you discover your own powerful solutions. We've all witnessed this happen or experienced it ourselves. A few suggestions to stimulate thinking—and in minutes, *breakthrough!*—a much better idea is born, custom-made by you and for you.

Designed for Change Leaders of Many Kinds

This book and the other *Diversity Breakthrough! Strategic Action Series* books and tools have been designed to be relevant to any organization, company or entity working to create a diverse, inclusive organization, workplace or community. I have been thinking of all of you as I have developed this body of work. It's inclusive. This seemed important for more than the obvious reason.

Admittedly, there are unique characteristics and differences in our organizations. We have different customers, missions and goals. We have different names for issues. We have different kinds of people doing the work. The work is different. However, at the core of all our efforts, the process of change is the same. It requires *assessment* of current realities, *acceptance* that there must be a better way and support for it, *action* to realize progress, *accountability* to give change meaning, recognition of *achievement* to fuel next steps and ultimately *more action.* This *perpetual cycle for achieving results* is common to all of us regardless if you are a large or small business, non-profit organization, school, university, church, government agency, military, community or any other entity.

This same *perpetual cycle of action* applies to the process of change necessary to fulfill our unique and individual goals for creating a diverse, inclusive organization. A lesson from Peter Drucker about organization design and structure can easily be applied to this challenge: A diverse, inclusive environment will not just evolve. It requires thinking, analysis and a systematic approach. Measuring progress and celebrating results will fuel ongoing achievements.

A Model for Achieving Results

The graphic model on the next page represents the *perpetual cycle of action* necessary to achieve results. It depicts the strategic action process of change described previously. In this book, it has been applied to creating a diverse, inclusive organization—but also it works for achieving results anywhere in your business. It has been the guide for this body of work. It is intentionally represented as an imperfect circle. Our efforts for change rarely go perfectly. Instead, they are journeys down unpaved, often winding roads. As Viktor Frankl shared in his book, *Man's Search for Meaning,* these uncharted paths of action are built *"from our personal dedication to a cause greater than we are."* Progress results in achievement. Achievement inspires more action.

Diversity Breakthrough! Perpetual Cycle of Action Model

The model below is not presented as something new. I'm a firm believer that there is nothing new—we have all we need. So, let's call it a tracing of what worked for me over the years as a manager and change leader—the logical sequence of steps we've all taken to achieve results in our own lives and work.

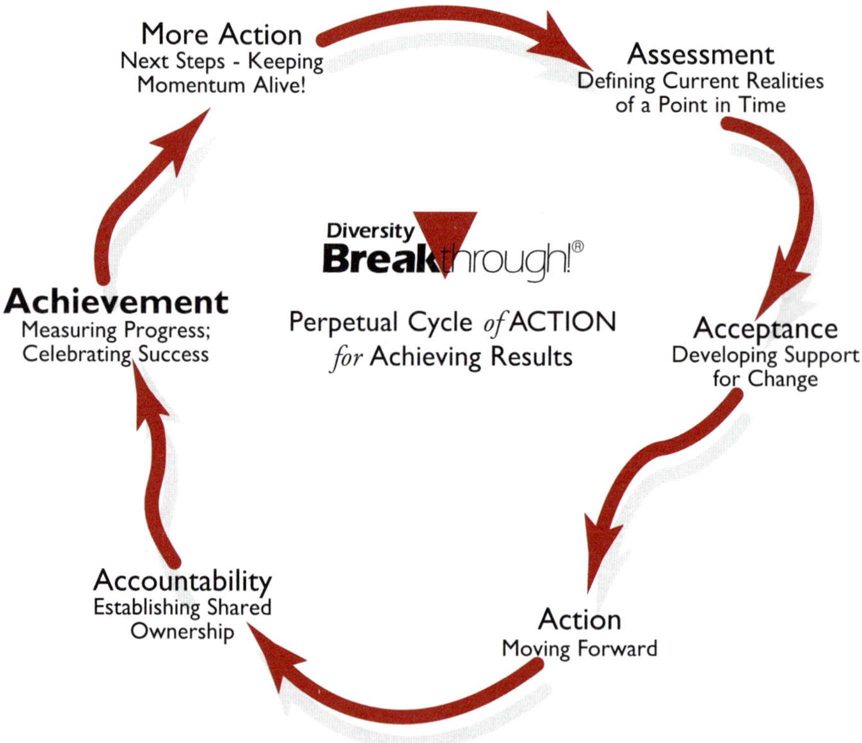

Starting

Setting Direction; Defining Actions

Whether you are launching a new diversity and inclusion initiative or you are working to renew and revitalize an existing effort, measuring progress and celebrating success are important ingredients. The following five-step process will get you started!

Step 1: Profiling Your Current Realities

The categories shown on the profile below represent key areas that have a significant influence on the overall effectiveness of creating a diverse, inclusive environment. For each category, select a number from 1–10 that best represents your organization's current level of effectiveness in measuring and celebrating success in each category based on your knowledge. On the vertical line above each category on the profile plot your level of effectiveness.

DIVERSITY & INCLUSION CURRENT REALITY PROFILE

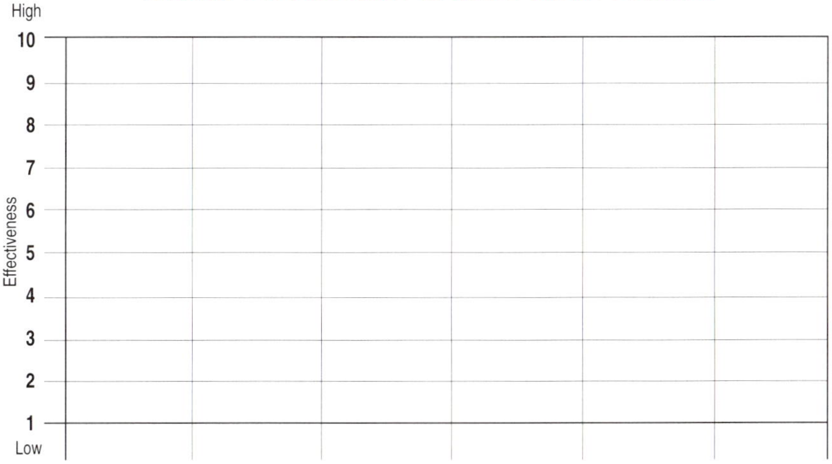

Leadership	Culture	Involvement	Business	Strategy & Measures	Staffing & Development	Ownership
• Involvement • Sponsorship • Diversity at all levels	• Value-based • Supports change	Participation at all levels from everybody	Readiness for multicultural, global realities, changing marketplace and community	• Vision • Strategy • Tactical plans • Measures • Systems • Compliance with regulations • Reviews	Diverse & Inclusive… • Hires • Promotions • Recognition • Development • Mentoring • Training	Standards established for individual contribution and recognition of them

Step 2: Forming Conclusions

Based on your *Diversity & Inclusion Current Reality Profile,* what factors did you consider as you evaluated your organization's effectiveness in measuring and celebrating achievement? Consider each category. Write a brief summary of your thoughts below:

PRIORITY

☐ Leadership

☐ Culture

☐ Involvement

☐ Business

☐ Strategy & Measures

☐ Staffing & Development

☐ Ownership

Step 3: Define Top Priorities

Review your summary on the adjacent page. Think about which areas are the greatest inhibitors to *moving* your diversity and inclusion initiatives *forward.* Think about those areas that if you could better measure and acknowledge achievements would have the greatest influence on creating momentum. Go back to *Step 2.* Rank issues in order of priority. Indicate your assigned priority for each category in the boxes on the left.

Step 4: Explore Self-Assessment Possibilities

Based on your ranked list of priorities, turn to the corresponding WHAT YOU CAN DO strategies sections to explore the possibilities for measuring and celebrating success. Worksheets are provided at the end of each of the sections to record your thinking and ideas on what approach you plan to take. When you complete your exploration, return to this page to complete *Step 5.*

Step 5: Define Goal-Directed Action—*Next Steps*

Based on your exploration of the WHAT YOU CAN DO *achievement* strategies, your own thinking and ideas and further refinement of priorities, what specific *next steps* are in order? You may find it most effective to create two or three doable *next steps.* ACT on them. Review results. Reassess what is needed next. Then define two to three new doable goals. This *perpetual cycle of action* will be a powerful force in accelerating change. Summarize your plan below. Work the plan.

DIVERSITY & INCLUSION GOAL-DIRECTED ACTION PLAN

Date	Description	Owner	Target Date

FOLLOW-ON GOAL DIRECTED ACTION PLAN

Date	Description	Owner	Target Date

Expanding the Dialogue—*Looking Deeper*

The most important next step may be to look more specifically into the key areas of influence you identified in your profile. Additionally, you may want to involve others on your team to help you validate your conclusions and refine priorities for next steps.

To take a closer look at the issues that are standing in the way of creating a diverse, inclusive environment, you may find the *Diversity Breakthrough! Action Dialogues: Meaningful Conversations to Accelerate Change* a helpful set of tools. Even if you have used it during other phases of change, the conversation will be different based on your current focus on measuring and celebrating success. It includes step-by-step processes for *three* different kinds of action-directed dialogues designed to help you define what is going well, where change is needed and what you are going to do about it. These meaningful conversations are not only productive, but they work as a catalyst for creating shared understanding, acceptance and ownership for change. *Diversity Breakthrough! Action Dialogues* comes with its own problem-identification tool. *Fifty-two* common issues are defined for you, categorized into the same seven areas of influence you profiled on page 11 *(leadership, culture, involvement, the business, strategies and measures, staffing and development, and ownership).*

For information on the *Diversity Breakthrough! Action Dialogues* and other books and tools in the *Diversity Breakthrough! Strategic Action Series,* turn to page 62.

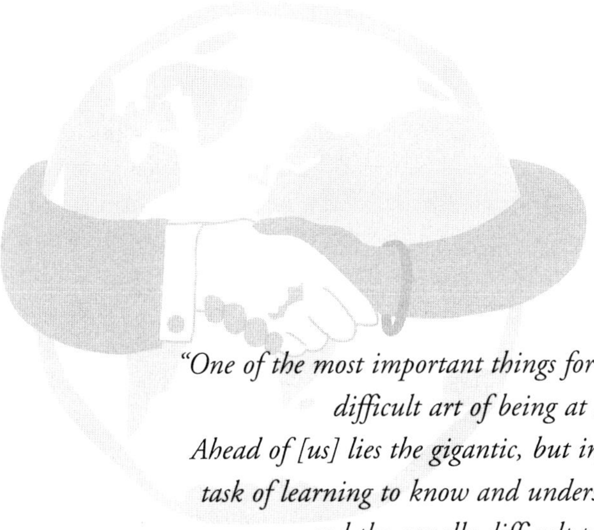

"One of the most important things for [us] to learn is the difficult art of being at home in the world. Ahead of [us] lies the gigantic, but infinitely rewarding, task of learning to know and understand other peoples, and the equally difficult task of helping other peoples to know and understand [us]."

—Eleanor Roosevelt
Former First Lady of the United States
and humanitarian

The Human Will to Change

... A Reflection

by Debbe Kennedy

We always remember the leaders who teach us by their example more than their words. This is a story of one leader that touched my life. His name was Bob. He was 24 years old with a promising future. Then, unexpectedly, life changed. He was in a motorcycle accident that left him a paraplegic. Bob and I met when he had been in his wheelchair only about 18 months. He was nominated for a computer programming training program at the *Resource Center for the Handicapped (RCH)* in Seattle. At the time, I worked for IBM, one of the sponsoring companies. Bob was one of our brightest students, but his growing anguish over his new reality was turning him into an embittered, belligerent, disrespectful, non-contributor in the program. The whole class was impacted by his acting out. After exhaustive counseling and coaching efforts, I was given the duty to inform him of his impending expulsion from the program. The moment—and his face—remain vivid in my memory. *"You have until Monday, Bob,"* I told him. *"You have until Monday to decide if changing and staying here is worth it to you."* He left in a screaming fury.

None of us knew what Monday would bring. I hoped. About five minutes before class started, I looked up and there he was. No words were spoken. We just looked at each other. We both heard in the silence, *"Please give me a chance."*

Bob went on to graduate *number two* in his class. He went to work for a major company as a programmer. He was promoted several times the first two years. More importantly, he volunteered his time, going back into the hospitals to become a role model for others. He brought hope to those searching to make sense of the new rules brought about with one of life's paradigm shifts. Soon he was named Washington State Volunteer of the Year. That year, there was a picture of Bob on the back of the RCH Annual Report. He was climbing the University of Washington climbing rock (I understand he was the first paraplegic to have this achievement). The caption read, *"The biggest engineering feat is that of human will."* This is the challenge we all have as leaders—to harness our human will to change and lead the way for others.

What You Can Do

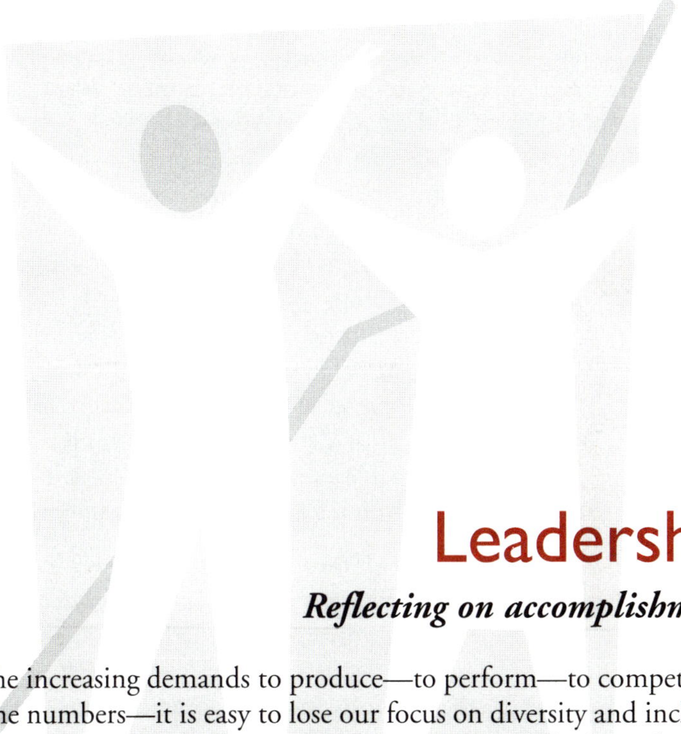

Leadership

Reflecting on accomplishments

With the increasing demands to produce—to perform—to compete—to make the numbers—it is easy to lose our focus on diversity and inclusion as leaders in any organization. It is even easier to overlook or disregard one of the major catalysts for renewing our day-to-day consciousness and commitment to keep moving forward—*reflection. "...trying to be good may be to stop running and take time to be quiet and discover who you are and where you have been,"* echoes the gentle counsel of Carmelite Nun, Sister Corita Kent. The pauses we make don't need to be long. Even a few moments can be powerful in shaping a new level of action. The WHAT YOU CAN DO strategy ideas and suggestions presented in this section are designed to foster your own thinking and actions on how you can:

- reflect on the past to build *bridges* to the next level of action,
- keep the big picture in view and perspectives in balance, and
- reward hard work with your personal reassurance.

Leadership

Reflecting on accomplishments

Success—progress, change, accomplishment—whatever you call it, big or seemingly small, is a moment in time that holds the knowledge and inspiration for leaders to move themselves and the organization to the next level in creating a diverse, inclusive environment. Most leaders do not recognize its power, and even fewer ever come close to tapping the potential that *success* has to help them seize the opportunity for new levels of innovation. *Success* knows the history of our journey, its mistakes, lessons and accomplishments. *Success* is a mirror from which one can see the future possibilities with greater clarity. It boosts our confidence, fosters new levels of trust, helps us make sound decisions and can spread a message like wildfire in the hands of a determined leader. Here are some ideas of what you can do to turn success into a leadership tool for ongoing change:

- **Honor the past.** Many leaders make big mistakes when they begin a new initiative for diversity and inclusion or begin to revitalize an existing one. There is always a tendency to close the door tight on anything related to the previous work, even when there is plenty of *life* in it. It is pretty safe to assume this happens routinely in other aspects of our organizational operations, too. This is particularly common when there has been a "changing of the guard" or a restructuring of some kind—someone leaves a post or the organization changes. Many of us commonly wipe out the past or quickly blanket it with our new ideas without really thinking through the implications. There are certainly benefits in a new and different message, but it's all in how you go about it. This is particularly true with issues around diversity and inclusion, where there is a fine line between moving ahead and falling back. Within what may appear to be *old stuff* to us lies the knowledge of the journey that came before us. Here are some ideas how to leverage the past, using it as a foundation for a new focused direction. 1) Remember, it is to your advantage to find "success" in previous work and use it to build a *bridge* to the next level of work. Good can always be found, if we are open to see it. If you instead completely trash the past, you send the message the last effort was a bomb—everyone's work made no difference. The time, energy and trust in it didn't matter. With that impression, you cast a shadow of uncertainty on your new initiative. *What makes your program any different from the last one that obviously didn't work?* 2) Dig through the files to find interesting pieces of data that will help you create the transition. It might be in the form of old flip charts, Post-It® notes, overhead slides, or perhaps you'll find something in an announcement package, a strategy folder or meeting binder. Look for things like statistical charts, feedback summaries, lists of issues, people's insights on values and vision, survey data, video messages or brochures. 3) Study what you find, looking for the highlights of the journey's early beginnings. 4) Compare then to now. Identify progress in a broad sense: Change in attitudes, lessons learned, numbers improved, people educated, awareness increased, programs initiated or even the experience of charting unknown territory together. Keep it simple and brief. 5) Use the highlights as a means of telling the story, creating the bridge for people to connect to the new initiative or refocused effort. Select a variety of types of data to appeal to different people. 6) Leave remnants of the past. For example, you may want to give logos, names, slogans an updated look and feel versus starting all over. There is great value in "brand" familiarity of your diversity and inclusion work, especially if you punctuate it with a message of past *success.* Your acknowledgement of past *success* gives instant credibility to the new work, even to those who were not particularly involved in it directly. It gives it the strength of history. 7) Be generous and genuine in giving predecessors and the people credit for their contributions that have enabled the organization to move on with a new level of diversity and inclusion focus. Remember, you minimize the impact of change, provide a sense of accomplishment and a springboard for the new work when you honor the important work from the past, whether it is your own or work from another leader.

• **Keep progress in the forefront.** Most of us like to measure and chart our progress. The validation of this surrounds our lives—anniversaries, report cards, scoreboards, quarterly reviews, birthdays or graduations to name a few examples. With this in mind, it is interesting how we forget this practice with our diversity and inclusion initiatives. What has not been done, needs to be done or wasn't done well enough seems to commonly get center stage. Isn't it the problems that get our attention and top billing at staff meetings, team meetings, roundtables and feedback sessions?

This is understandable. Progress is slow. There remains so much left to do—and so little time. However, I think most of us would agree, the *what have you done for me lately* approach is discouraging when you are on the receiving end. As leaders, there is an easy remedy to keep issues and progress in balance for yourself and everyone else. 1) Let *what's right* be the prelude to all thinking or talking before moving on to *what's wrong.* 2) Work to make this a personal *habit* and help others do the same. It will take discipline, because we have some old, crusty habits to break. We have evolved into *bottom-line* society in a rush, so we fast forward, bypass, minimize or belittle the symbols of progress by ignoring them, showing our disinterest in them or overshadowing all accomplishments by casting negative energy on them. Many of us have this practice so ingrained in our being, we aren't even comfortable talking about achievements. We have made statements of doubt, complaints or negatively posed questions the basis for communication. 3) Look for opportunities to incorporate this *what's right prelude* in your day-to-day meetings and conversations. With practice, it will become second nature. Regularly acknowledging *what's right—what's been accomplished*—changes the dynamics of conversations and our whole perspective. It helps us see the big picture. It is a source of encouragement and it keeps our view of things balanced. Most of all, it helps us fulfill our human need to feel what we are doing is worthwhile and instills us with the courage to persevere. You may find *Diversity Breakthrough! Action Dialogues* a valuable tool to help you master this technique. Refer to page 62.

- **Reward the champions with your reassurance.** The goals for diversity and inclusion have been slow in coming and they take hard work on many levels. A West Point cadet's message about leadership in Warren Bennis' video *The Leader Within* reminds us of the importance of *reassurance.* He told of how good it felt to have a senior cadet down in the sawdust with you saying, *"Stay with me. Keep going. Always stay with me."* His conclusion, *"It's a lot different having someone push you, than having someone lead you." Reassurance* is a form of reflection and recognition that the cause or objective you are working to achieve matters—and you are not alone. Be generous with it.

Using past successes to build *bridges* to next steps, imprinting *how far we've come* and giving people a compelling reason to keep going are essential roles for leaders creating diverse, inclusive organizations. Use the MEASURING PROGRESS; CELEBRATING SUCCESS—*Leadership* exercise on the adjacent page to help you reflect on these ideas, think through your own and formulate plans for action.

Measuring Progress; Celebrating Success—Leadership

Which ideas might be helpful to you?

- ☐ Honor the past.
- ☐ Keep progress in the forefront.
- ☐ Reward the champions with your reassurance.

For more LEADERSHIP strategy ideas see the supporting books and tools in the *Diversity Breakthrough! Strategic Action Series.* To learn more, see page 62.

What ideas do you have for next steps?

What ACTION will you take? ✔ Done

Date ☐

Date ☐

Date ☐

Date ☐

Date ☐

Add a summary of your plans to your *Diversity & Inclusion Goal-Directed Action Plan* on page 13.

Smiles Are Passports
... A Story

Catherine DeVrye
Author, *Good Service Is Good Business, Japan: An A to Z* and *The Customer Service Zoo*
1993 Australian Executive Woman of the Year

The more I travel, the more I realize that people are the same. There are distinct differences in terms of ways of doing business and cultural sensitivities, but there are more similarities between people than differences. We share similar hopes and fears. Basically, we all want to have the finest possible lifestyle for our families and do our own personal best to gain job satisfaction and enough money to enjoy our leisure. At work, we share the same frustrations of not enough hours in the day, too much bureaucracy, internal politics, computers that break or mobile phones that are out of range. Even if some of us have never heard of a cell phone, we are still subject to changing conditions in our external environments over which they have no control, whether it be trade sanctions or floods that wipe out an annual crop.

Coming from a country of 20 million Downunder, I've been apprehensive about speaking in India, Korea, Indonesia—even Edinburgh or Fort Collins. Will they have the same sense of humor as audiences in Sydney? Are the issues the same? Will my thoughts be relevant? Inevitably, fears are allayed, in spite of the in-flight magazine being in a totally different language and, perhaps, being served marinated eel for breakfast.

Don't be concerned if you never really understand everything about doing business globally. You probably never will. But, it is better to know what you do not know and have an open mind than to think you understand what you really do not. Certainly there are different value systems, and some countries are more spiritualistic than materialistic, but even these goals don't need to be mutually exclusive. Whether it is a toothless smile from an old man at the base of the Great Wall of China, or the pearly whites of an eight-year-old in Kenya, I am constantly reminded of the universality of the human race.

As a little girl, my grandfather used to tell me, *"A smile is a frown turned upside down."* His only travel was when he migrated from Scotland to Canada at the turn of the last century. He would marvel at the changes in today's world but the one thing hasn't changed—*smiles are still passports through deserts and visas to all foreign countries.*

What You Can Do

Culture

Celebrating diversity, inclusion & renewal

There is a movement gaining momentum. More and more organizations across industries and sectors are recognizing that creating a culture that values diversity and inclusion is essential to their future success. The wake-up call can be credited to the sacrifices and determination of many people working tirelessly to get our attention and raise our consciousness, as well as from the emerging realities of a global marketplace and a global society that are changing work and life as we know it. There is much left to do and many people left to convince, but the opportunity and resources we need to continue the work have never been so plentiful—the message so compelling and far-reaching. This is an achievement! The WHAT YOU CAN DO strategy ideas and suggestions presented in this section are designed to foster your own thinking and actions on how you can:

- strengthen community and relationships with your successes,
- use achievements to foster recommitment on many levels, and
- celebrate achievements in a way that fits the culture.

Culture

Celebrating diversity, inclusion & renewal

As people and as organizations, we all have our unique perspectives on diversity and inclusion. The way we approach it, the words we use and the levels of progress we achieve are measured by our own unique standards. We may respond to the movement toward a diverse, inclusive environment for different reasons and be driven by different intentions—but the common goal is continuous improvement and renewal. As we enter the 21st Century never has it been more possible and more critical to our future. Here are some ideas of what YOU can do to use celebration and renewal to influence new levels of change:

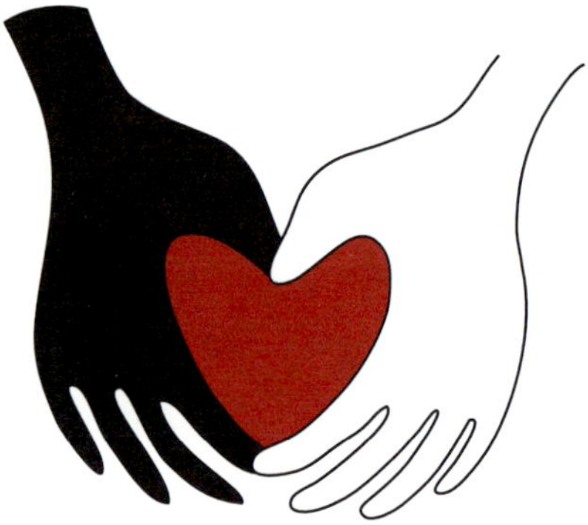

• **Strengthen community with success.** We all like to be part of a successful endeavor. Take the time to see how far you have come. Take time to look around, review the facts and figures and reflect on where you started and what has changed. Look for new attitudes, participation and levels of understanding. Think about what processes, programs and other activities shaped the journey. Then, talk about it. Get others talking about it. Use a few ideas from your observations and let the people fill in the blanks. A time of reflection—recognition of how far you have come—will not happen on its own. The process of looking back will inspire renewal. Renewal is the catalyst for *more action.* An organization that shares in this common experience will be stronger. It doesn't have to be a major event. It can be a little time at staff meetings quarterly. It could be an e-mail conversation, where everyone inputs and results are sent to everyone. It can also be a more formal review session. Refer to page 62 for other *Diversity Breakthrough!* books and tools that may be helpful to you based on your level of progress.

• **Connect with sponsors.** Many times we only come to our sponsors in times of need or crisis. Take the time to keep them informed, engaged and enthused about your progress toward creating a diverse, inclusive environment. Help them see the good being accomplished every chance you get. Here are a few practices that will help you do this: 1) Keep your own eyes open to see small victories. 2) Make connecting with sponsors practice. 3) Make it your business to have a few key indicators of ready to share when the opportunity presents itself. 4) Use these oppor to give sponsors a sense of accomplishment about their contributio , as well as a means of strengthening your relationship.

• **Take it to the board.** Organizational diversity and inclusion success stories probably don't make many board meeting agendas, but they should. The experts agree that PEOPLE will be the competitive advantage in the 21st Century, regardless of the marketplace or community you serve. The fact that organizational culture is a key success factor in attracting, developing and retaining the best people indicates that creating a diverse, inclusive environment would be a priority no one on the board would intentionally overlook. Here are some ideas to consider: 1) Since this kind of conversation may be a new one, design your presentation to be compelling and brief with a clear link to the specific bottom line your board cares about. 2) Give them more than statistics. Make the data come alive with the stories to support the numbers—stories that are shaping new levels of organizational success. 3) Use this opportunity as a platform to raise consciousness about the board's role in ensuring it also reflects the marketplace, community and the organization in its representation. 4) Create a premise, approach and message that you believe in and find value in yourself. Your goal is not only engaging the board, but also selling yourself and others that diversity and inclusion belong on the agenda. 5) Don't get discouraged if your early attempts fail. It may take time to convince others. There is always a *right* time that will emerge and you will be prepared to respond. When you engage the board in your success, you will have made a major inroad in expanding your realm of influence.

• **Celebrate differences and cultures.** As your organization begins to be a reflection of a diverse and inclusive place, find ways to celebrate it, while learning more about each other. This can help you develop a deeper understanding, acceptance of differences and a glimpse inside the cultures represented in the marketplace and community you serve. It is important to pick some format that works for your organization's style and situation, but it could be as simple as an informal multicultural feast you all contribute to preparing, a cultural study group or reading group, or perhaps it is independently taking a course and then having a dialogue about learning. You will find many ideas for expanding your achievements through cross-cultural learning and celebration in these suggested books:

Diversity Success Strategies by Norma Carr-Ruffino
Creating Community Anywhere by Carolyn R. Shaffer & Kristin Anundsen
Feeding the Body, Nourishing the Soul by Deborah Kesten
Celebrations Around the World by Carole S. Angell
Multicultural Manners by Norine Dresser

• **Renew your team covenant.** Whether it is formal or informal, if you are celebrating success, some code of behavior and actions has emerged. Make renewing or creating a team agreement part of your celebration. It helps everyone see how far you have come, while sharing in the experience of recommitment to your values and vision of a more diverse, inclusive organization.

• **Celebrate in silence.** The measurement of whether we have created a diverse, inclusive environment is often understood more by what is seen, felt, sensed and experienced than by numbers or what is said. If you have worked or lived in such a welcoming place, no words are particularly necessary—nor capable of describing what you know from *being* in it. Here are a few celebrations to be done in silence: 1) Smile more. It is a way to spread contentment. 2) Take a mental inventory each day of how you contributed to creating a diverse, inclusive organization. This personal ritual will help you stay focused. 3) Send an e-mail to a co-worker to tell them you are glad they are on the team or in appreciation of something they have contributed. 4) Take *one minute* regularly to look out and around and feel a sense of gratitude for the people and the community of which you are a part. 5) Think about what you might do to help others cultivate these habits of reflection and action. *Success* is often a very quiet place inside us with a powerful capability to radiate outward to others. Help it.

Changing the mindset of a culture is a major achievement. Every step in the right direction deserves acknowledgement. Use the MEASURING PROGRESS; CELEBRATING SUCCESS—*Culture* exercise on the adjacent page to help you reflect on these ideas, think through your own and formulate plans for action.

Measuring Progress; Celebrating Success—Culture:

Which ideas might be helpful to you?

- ☐ Strengthen community with success.
- ☐ Connect with sponsors.
- ☐ Take it to the board.
- ☐ Celebrate differences and cultures.
- ☐ Renew your team covenant.
- ☐ Celebrate in silence.

For more CULTURE strategy ideas see the supporting books and tools in the *Diversity Breakthrough! Strategic Action Series.* To learn more, see page 62.

What ideas do you have for next steps?

____

____

____

____

____

What ACTION will you take? ✔ Done

______________________________ Date ______ ☐

______________________________ Date ______ ☐

______________________________ Date ______ ☐

______________________________ Date ______ ☐

______________________________ Date ______ ☐

Add a summary of your plans to your *Diversity & Inclusion Goal-Directed Action Plan* on page 13.

Bringing People Together
... *A Story*

J. T. (Ted) Childs, Jr.
Vice President, Global Workforce Diversity
IBM Corporation

There are signs of people coming together all over the world—gatherings that might not have happened at one time. As an example, recently I attended the *Leadership Conference for Civil Rights Dinner* in Washington D.C. The *Leadership Conference* represents a coming together of all of the civil rights organizations—*minority, gender, gay/lesbian, aging and others*—under one roof to form an alliance, because they are all fighting for something—fairness and equal treatment for themselves and each other.

We have seen the same kind of energy emerge as our various diversity councils within the company have been formed—people coming together to help us better understand the issues as a company and better understand each other around the world, so we can have the best possible team representing IBM in the marketplace to support our diverse customers.

As we have been working to reinforce the link between our workplace and our marketplace at IBM, we have discovered opportunities to bring people together we had overlooked. For example, we had situations where people tried to buy from us and couldn't: A man from Mexico once called the 800 number and there wasn't anyone on duty that spoke Spanish. He had called to place an order. We had four people who worked in the call center that spoke Spanish, but they weren't on duty. Having someone that speaks Spanish on duty all the time is helping us make connections.

We have also recognized as we are building a global culture of inclusion that it means, no matter who you are at IBM, you will have to work with co-workers and customers who are different from you—*black, white, brown, red or yellow, young or old, gay or straight, male or female, able bodied or physically challenged.* People who don't live in your neighborhood. People who don't pray in your church. People who don't come from where you come from. Working here means respecting the diversity we represent.

There are signs of progress that at one time were just dreams—and it makes this work very rewarding. One thing that really makes me feel good inside is bringing people together—all people.

What You Can Do

Involvement

Recognizing contributions; fueling next steps

Creating a diverse, inclusive environment for most of us is a constant task of *pioneering*. It is a continual work-in-progress by everyone in an organization—each of us doing our part to forge the new way in uncharted, ever-changing territory. There is no map—just our relentless, collective pursuit of a better way. Our journey is much like the one Kazuo Inamori, Founder and Chairman Emeritus of Kyocera Corporation in Japan, shares in his book, *Passion for Success*. *"...mine was a sea of uncharted territory. There was no lighthouse....I had to make a lighthouse of myself to illuminate the way."* This is our challenge. Our achievements keep our lights brightly shining, so others can join us and help us find the way. The WHAT YOU CAN DO strategy ideas and suggestions presented in this section are designed to foster your own thinking and actions on how you can:

- creatively approach the notion of celebration,
- invite individuals, networks and teams to participate, and
- inspire new action with a perpetual cycle of success.

Involvement

Recognizing contributions; fueling next steps

Keeping people involved and committed in creating a diverse and inclusive organization is an ongoing challenge for most organizations—success is a major catalyst. It is important to openly recognize contributions, role models that inspire us and use our achievements—*even small wins*—to create the sense of progress. Success renews our sense of purpose in the continuing journey. Without this, people lose interest, get discouraged and give up. Successes are the milestones that boost our spirits and inject us with the courage we need to move on to the next set of challenges. Here are some ideas of what YOU can do to acknowledge contributions and fuel new levels of achievement:

- **Engage your network and support groups.** Many formal and informal support groups are emerging in organizations and much good is being done. Involve the groups in creating a *Reader's Theatre* centered around how the organization is changing—and how lives have been influenced by the concerted effort to create a more diverse, inclusive environment. This would in itself be a celebration and a collective show of gratitude for the progress everyone has made possible. It would also help renew everyone's commitment to more action at all levels of the organization. All you need is willing people, a collection of stories to share and representative examples of progress, perhaps linked to one or more of the seven areas of influence represented in this book. This will give your script a broader appeal, because it will touch multiple aspects of organizational success. Refer to page 11 to review all seven areas. You can learn about the basic principles of creating a script at the library and on the Internet. Search *reader's theater* or *storytelling.* One helpful resource is *Aaron Shepard's Reading Theatre* page at *www.aaronshep.com/rt.* You might want to do multiple performances —obviously, *live* is best, but it also may be worth creating a video of it as you master the technique. Share it with the board and your executive team. Create a simple discussion process that goes with it to help managers use it with their teams. A Reader's Theater would make an interesting story for newsletters, a creative web shop or teleconference and an inspiring way to share your stories, as well as help others recognize the value of everyone's hard work. When everyone, at all levels, can see the success of diversity and inclusion and feel part of it, it gives us all a compelling reason to *stay* involved—or *get* involved when we may have previously been sitting on the sidelines.

• **Redefine celebrations.** Perhaps our first thoughts when we think about a celebration of diversity and inclusion achievements is about having a party, a recognition event or some other forum where we all get together. You can't beat *being* together to share best practices and stories of success. However, as technology continues to bring us closer and closer together, new ways to *celebrate* are becoming possible. Here are some considerations: 1) Explore the possibilities for web shops, teleconferencing, chat rooms and online auditoriums as opportunities to keep a perpetual cycle of success and communication opening the way. 2) Format your celebration, so people have a chance to *dialogue* about what progress has been made and how those changes are manifesting themselves in their work and lives. 3) If you also want to get input for your next steps, give it a positive *spin* to make it more productive and avoid it turning into a gripe session. For example, say you want to get feedback on what the issues are now. Here is a positive way to ask for that input, *"What top issue should we take on now? How do you think resolving this issue will contribute to organizational success? What would success look like? What are you personally willing to contribute?"* This approach says, *"We want your input, ideas and participation in success."*

• **Create a celebration video.** Find diversity and inclusion in your organizational successes and create a video of representative perspectives from teams and individuals. If you can't afford a professional video crew, don't feel left out—home video equipment can do the job. The idea is to capture people talking *from the heart* about what has changed, what it has meant to them and how it is benefiting *customers.* Again the seven areas of influence on page 11 may serve as a guide for identifying success stories. Here are a few considerations on what to do: 1) Give people the questioning themes to think through, but *no scripts.* 2) Conduct the interviews. 3) Have the best segments edited together. 4) Give your video a name. 5) Create a lead-in. 6) Use it as a *backdrop* for team dialogue and celebration—or use it as an opening for a more formal celebration. 7) Invite everyone to share in it by adding their stories.

• **Integrate your celebrations.** Honoring achievements doesn't always have to be associated with a dedicated diversity and inclusion event. Develop a simple discussion format and process that could easily be incorporated or used by teams to talk about what is going *right* and how they are serving their *customers* better because of it. The U.S. Army is doing this with their *Consideration of Others* program as a continuous means of keeping communication lines open, encouraging mutual understanding of each member of the unit, as well as improving team performance. It is modeled after their *After Action Review* process that focuses on *what's going right, what's going wrong* and *what can we do to get better.*

You can learn more in "Consideration for Others," a story by Major Jan Swicord, U.S. Army in the *Diversity Breakthrough! Assessment: Defining Current Realities* book, page 28.

• **Publish your success story.** Look back at your vision and values and trace your journey. Identify someone on the team that is willing to take a stab at writing the story—or even a poem. Here are some ideas and considerations: 1) Have people e-mail or fax one example of how your focus on creating a diverse, inclusive organization has made a difference. 2) Integrate highlights of the input into your story. If you are a small team, try to acknowledge everyone in some way. If you are a larger team, select cross-functional representation that shows you were thinking about your entire organizational family. 3) Ask a person of influence in the organization to write a *Foreword* for the story. 4) Put it on your website. 5) Read it at a team meeting. 6) Turn it into an article for a newsletter. 7) Creatively lay it out. Give everyone a copy. 8) Let your mind go on the possibilities of how your story might help you engage others and fuel next steps.

• **Make your web an ongoing celebration of success.** Here are a few ideas to stimulate your own thinking: 1) Get on the *editorial calendar* for features to celebrate people making a difference—perhaps once a quarter or twice a year. 2) Create a diversity and inclusion *hall of fame.* Add new stories every month. 3) Make them short and inspiring. 4) Bring them to life with pictures or graphics. 5) Make success stories a main menu selection.

Keeping people involved requires ongoing encouragement and a vision of success that keeps unfolding. Use the MEASURING PROGRESS; CELEBRATING SUCCESS—*Involvement* exercise on the adjacent page to help you reflect on these ideas, think through your own and formulate plans for action.

MEASURING PROGRESS; CELEBRATING SUCCESS—Involvement:

Which ideas might be helpful to you?

- ☐ Engage your network and support groups.
- ☐ Redefine celebrations.
- ☐ Create a celebration video.
- ☐ Integrate your celebrations.
- ☐ Publish your success story.
- ☐ Make your web an ongoing celebration of success.

For more INVOLVEMENT strategy ideas see the supporting books and tools in the *Diversity Breakthrough! Strategic Action Series.* To learn more, see page 62.

What ideas do you have for next steps?

____

____

____

____

____

What ACTION will you take?

		✔ Done
____________________	Date ______	☐
____________________	Date ______	☐
____________________	Date ______	☐
____________________	Date ______	☐
____________________	Date ______	☐

Add a summary of your plans to your *Diversity & Inclusion Goal-Directed Action Plan* on page 13.

New Language for Success
… A Story

Emily Duncan
Director, Global Diversity & Work/Life
Hewlett-Packard Company

We have traveled a long distance. Signs of progress can be seen every day. Yet, there is much left to be done. Now, I think we need to come up with some new language for *diversity.* The language we have used to get us where we are has been very helpful. However, to connect with our rapidly changing organizations, we need a new message that helps everyone recognize and understand the issue being addressed today is about business success and workplace effectiveness. It centers around how to get things done better with different perspectives, different people and different ideas. The focus of our conversations also needs to change. Instead of talking about what is different—*diversity*—we need to shift our discussions to how we can work together to find ways to use our differences to effectively solve our customers' problems.

There have been significant benefits in investing our time and resources to get people ready, letting them know a change was coming. We had to help everyone get used to the emerging realities in every workplace and community—that people who look, think, act, live and feel differently would soon be around and part of our common everyday experience. We have had that conversation, and I believe we really need to move on with the message, "*We told you change was coming. Now it's here. Now we need to be clear about what we need to do to ensure we are all successful.*"

Organizations are going to have to hold on to core values as they move forward quickly—with a focus on people. Unless our people have the best resources, the best environment, the best tools to produce whatever products and services we are making, selling or offering, it will be difficult as an organization to reach for success. We have to recognize that there are a lot of different people with very different needs today. To achieve this balance, I think we have to do two things. First, we must seize this opportunity for innovation by helping everyone understand how having a diverse workforce will help serve customers better and achieve new levels of results. Second, we have to respond to the demands of change, being flexible and agile enough to meet the needs of a variety of different people. These are essential building blocks to sustain success, so everyone can benefit from it. These are the achievements that will shape our destiny.

What You Can Do

The Business

Connecting the best in people with results achieved

There are new leadership messages emerging as companies and organizations are making the business connection to creating a diverse, inclusive organization. *"Not only is diversity good social policy, it is also an important business and competitive advantage—one we will pursue as zealously as we do other strategic initiatives,"* reported Arthur Martinez, Chairman and CEO of Sears, Roebuck and Co. as an example. The business success stories are mounting. *"Diversifying our staff is not some side project,"* reported Knight Ridder's *San Jose Mercury News* publisher, Jay Harris, *"It's a core part of our business strategy."* Knight Ridder was named as one of FORTUNE's 1999 top fifty *diversity elite* companies. How are your achievements influencing organizational success? The WHAT YOU CAN DO strategy ideas and suggestions presented in this section are designed to foster your own thinking and actions on how you can:

- begin to correlate organizational success with diversity success,
- celebrate with best practices and sharing results achieved, and
- build upon success with a little creativity.

The Business

Connecting the best in people with results achieved

The *business reasons* for creating diverse, inclusive organizations have been calling to us for a long time. It is true that we have not always had the driving forces of globalization and information technology *pushing* us into action across industries and sectors, but the opportunity to innovate—to add creativity and stability to our workforce and workplace—to make people our *business* advantage no matter how you define your marketplace has been there all along. Obviously, the hard work is paying off for your organization. Here are some ideas of what YOU can do to measure, celebrate and discover how diversity and inclusion links to organizational results:

- **Look for the correlation.** Regardless whether your business measurements are student achievement, communities served or products and services sold, what we have in common is serving our *customers.* Go behind the measurements on your organizational *scorecard* to see if you can see a difference in organizational performance as you have strengthened your team with diversity and created a more welcoming place. First, look for indicators in your organization that are the equivalent to increased revenue, new *markets* opened, increased *customer* satisfaction, results that came from team innovations or recognition received for superior service or achievement. Then, look for the people corollaries such as improved employee satisfaction, increased representation at all levels, more diverse teams, broader range of expertise and skills, expanded development and training. Compare the two to see if you can begin making the connection. Like planting a garden, the *seeds* of our actions to create a diverse, inclusive environment to better serve *customers* takes time to *sprout.* In the meantime, we need to *water* them with our continued action, while exploring the direct link to organizational success that will help us reach new levels of achievement however we define it.

- **Have senior leaders share their best practices.** Find out how teams are integrating diversity and inclusion into mainstream business. Ask team leaders to share at least one success story that demonstrates their efforts and tells how it is making a difference. Give them an outline for the story to make it easy for them to respond. Here are some ideas of what might be included: 1) A description of the success (i.e., innovation, problem solved, market opened). 2) Who was involved? 3) What obstacles were overcome? 4) What innovations have been realized? 5) What learnings about diversity and inclusion have emerged? 6) What recommendations, advice and counsel would you pass on to others? Here are a few ideas about how you might use these best practices to honor achievements and inspire others: Use the stories to help and encourage others. Add them to your website. Send them one at a time as part of senior management communications, including an acknowledgement of the achievement and a call-to-action for others. Use them as topics for team meetings or discussions. Invite the leaders and teams to share their stories at team meetings.

• **Let results speak for itself.** Expand your thinking about "business measures" to include measurements that reflect your progress toward your goals for creating a diverse, inclusive organization. For example, if your goals included improving employee satisfaction, expanding leadership development and increasing representation at all levels of your organization, post summaries of results to your business record. This might include scores from your employee survey, number of new volunteers, names of people attending a leadership development program, new hires or people promoted and *customer* success stories, for example. Then, create a *success* display on your bulletin board or website. Display both your business results and other achievements representing people-related accomplishments that are contributing to the organization expanding its capabilities to better serve *customers.* You may not initially see the correlations in the data, but as you all get used to seeing results integrated into one organization *success* profile, the interrelationship will certainly begin to emerge. Just the fact that you are bringing these measurements together—putting them on a par with revenue and other key measurements—will go a long way in helping everyone see the importance you place on your goals for diversity and inclusion and how they are an integral part of organizational success.

• **Show off your creativity.** You may be taking actions no one ever celebrates as an achievement and, consequently, rarely connects to your strategies to create a diverse, inclusive organization to better serve your customers. *What are you doing that should be acknowledged as a success strategy?* Remember, sharing the good news gives people a sense of purpose and progress. Here are some examples of the creative ways that organizations are making the business connection.

Lucent Technologies—Employees teach at colleges that graduate African-American engineers, an investment in growing and nurturing top talent for the future.

Allstate—Puts focus on revitalizing neighborhoods. Happy homeowners are great prospective customers.

Brooks United Methodist Church—Ushers use a smile, a welcoming demeanor and a distinctive white uniform to greet churchgoers, making a visible statement about the importance they place on making their *customers* feel included.

Sony Electronics—Puts an emphasis on "local globalization." Whenever possible they incorporate local practices in its work culture.

National Organization on Disability—Established a CEO Council to recognize business leaders for their support of people with disabilities in the workforce, inspiring leaders, building awareness, sponsors and potential sources of job opportunities.

U.S. Central Intelligence Agency—Offers internships to grow new talent in key staffing areas.

Brownard Hospital District—Director of Cultural Diversity writes an article for the *South Florida Business Journal* on the relationship of cultural diversity and good customer service. Sharing a valuable message, while making a statement that diversity matters at *Brownard.*

Cherry Semiconductor—Has a history of hiring international students as a means of broadening the diversity of its technical workforce; employees become sponsors for students after their first year of work. They grow talent and mentors.

We are rapidly finding the business connections to diversity success. They have been there all along. Use the MEASURING PROGRESS; CELEBRATING SUCCESS—*The Business* exercise on the adjacent page to help you reflect on these ideas, think through your own and formulate plans for action.

Measuring Progress; Celebrating Success—The Business:

Which ideas might be helpful to you?

- ☐ Look for the correlation.
- ☐ Have senior leaders share their best practices.
- ☐ Let results speak for itself.
- ☐ Show off your creativity.

For more Business strategy ideas see the supporting books and tools in the *Diversity Breakthrough! Strategic Action Series.* To learn more, see page 62.

What ideas do you have for next steps?

____

____

____

____

____

____

What action will you take? ✔ Done

______________________ Date ________ ☐

______________________ Date ________ ☐

______________________ Date ________ ☐

______________________ Date ________ ☐

______________________ Date ________ ☐

Add a summary of your plans to your *Diversity & Inclusion Goal-Directed Action Plan* on page 13.

Achievement Without Numbers

... *A Story*

David H. Ohle
Lieutenant General, U.S. Army
Deputy Chief of Staff for Personnel

For all organizations, creating and maintaining an environment where your beliefs in diversity and inclusion are realized is an ongoing process. With these human dimensions of leadership, results take many forms and some are not easy to quantify. For us, as an example, going back to *basics* to reinvigorate Army values is certainly one achievement. Another has been forging our *After Action Review*—a feedback process that helps us get better at everything we do—so this familiar and proven process can also help us measure individual leadership effectiveness. These are important steps, because we know it is individual leaders at all ranks that are building an environment of inclusion.

However, beyond values and supporting processes and programs, I think all our achievements as organizations will also come through innovations that will change traditional hierarchical and career patterns. For us, we know in the future, given the environment, the Army can no longer have the luxury to grow generalists. We have to rely on specialists, allowing for an expanded group of officers to do what they do best in their field of specialty. In response to this need, the Army has opened three new additional specialized career fields. This change benefits the Army in two ways: It strengthens the Army's capability with highly specialized expertise in every facet of Army operations, and it also broadens opportunities for promotion for our officers. We are not changing the culture of the Army—we have reshaped the structure. The Army of the 21st Century will be diverse at all ranks, with new perspectives and levels of expertise to support all aspects of our mission.

The Army is people—and the future is bright. Our greatest achievement is attracting, training, developing and keeping QUALITY people. I am truly honored to be the Deputy Chief of Staff for Personnel with responsibility for programs that take care of the Army's QUALITY people. Our leaders' success is the reward.

What You Can Do

Strategies & Measures

Focusing on accomplishments

As the 21st Century unfolds, we have an opportunity to redirect our thinking and our strategies about how to achieve a diverse, inclusive environment—in the marketplace, in the workplace, in every organization and community. We must learn from what we have achieved and ready ourselves for the opportunities to innovate that await us. This means having a willingness to see the issues with new eyes, elevating and sharpening our vision into one that serves us all. It means not allowing ourselves to be mired in every aspect of our individual differences, but instead recognizing and accepting the wealth and innovation that they hold—and putting it to work. The WHAT YOU CAN DO strategy ideas and suggestions presented in this section are designed to foster your own thinking and actions on how you can:

- reflect on your accomplishments and measure success,
- help others inside and outside do the same, and
- revitalize your journey with new thinking and courage.

Strategies & Measures

Focusing on accomplishments

Strategies and measures are frequently celebrated most before we have accomplished a thing. When the strategic model and its accompanying plan are unveiled, presentations are made, interviews are conducted and copies are sent to everyone important—and today, dazzling new website pages proclaim the new vision and direction. It seems safe to assume that commonly our strategies for creating a diverse, inclusive environment are given a similar treatment. Interestingly, when we work our hearts out to achieve our goals—changing minds, recruiting diverse talent to better serve our customers, increasing representation at all levels of the organization, championing successful programs, changing lives—there is little or no acknowledgement of these milestones. And we wonder why we get discouraged, lose momentum and struggle to get up for the next round of action. We lose a valuable source of energy, if we don't take a minute to take in the *thrill of victory* when it comes along—a moment for ourselves and for the organization. Nelson Mandela reminded all of us of the significance of this respite in the final words of *Long Walk to Freedom*, *"...I have taken a moment here to rest, to steal a view of the glorious vista that surrounds me, to look back on the distance I have come. But I can rest only for a moment, for with freedom come responsibilities, and I dare not linger, for my long walk is not yet ended."* Here are some ideas of what YOU can do to focus in on your accomplishments and help others do the same:

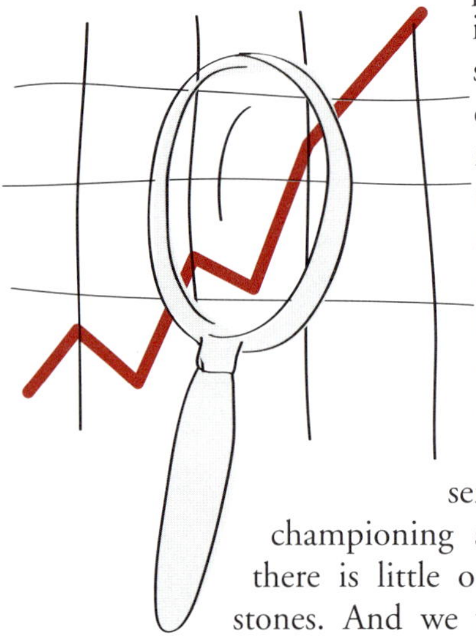

- **Compare your vision with reality.** Invest a little time looking closely at your initial vision. Select a small group with a flair for creativity and insightfulness. Have them examine your vision and brainstorm the ways your vision has begun to be manifested in the organization and the way it operates. You may want to give them a list of the *seven areas of influence* discussed on page 11 as a guide. Tailor the areas of influence so they fit your own organizational language, and provide the group with a few examples that demonstrate the kind of input you want to receive. This will give the group a premise from which to begin their exploration. Involving people in the organization in the exercise has a meaningful purpose. Recognizing successes is often more impactful and believable, if the successes are discovered by the people themselves. Ask them also to recommend one or two breakthrough next steps to help the organization move closer to fulfilling the vision. When the work is complete, use the findings in as many creative ways you can to spread the message of progress. Here are some ideas: 1) Have the team share the results at a celebration meeting; 2) Put it in a newsletter. 3) Write a story of the journey for your annual report. 4) Present an overview to the board; 5) Use the data for updating your business plan. 6) Write a press release or feature article that shares your victories and learnings, big and small. 7) Have other teams use it as a backdrop for dialogue. Let them add their perspectives to make it their own. 8) Prepare a card with the *highlights* of your successes on it. Make it a kind of keepsake to remember the hard work. Give one to everyone.

• **Celebrate with pictures.** Remember, *a picture is worth a thousand words.* Pictures also provide symbols of who we are and what we care about—they also help us connect with each other—see our reflection in an organization or community. Regardless of the type of organization you are, welcome your *customers,* prospective partners, volunteers and employees by letting them connect with who you have grown to be. Let them learn how your organization is finding strength in its diversity. Create a website or update the one you have with profiles of the people in your organization. Here are a few considerations: 1) Use pictures and a little creativity (candid or informal ones are best). 2) Add a personal highlight or two about the people to make a human connection. 3) Include a brief quote or message from each person you profile that tells about them, a perspective about your organization or, perhaps, an invitational-type message to your customers. 4) Work to give your website a new, welcoming, *alive* feeling for your visitors. This doesn't mean flashy. It means reaching beyond products and services to add a touch of humanness. *Remember,* people want to do business with organizations that can understand and relate to their needs—who have people like them. To see an example of what can be done, here are three sites where people pictures have impact: 1) the diversity pages on IBM's website at *www.ibm.com;* click on About IBM, search *diversity.* 2) Levi Strauss at *www.levistrauss.com.* 3) Glide Memorial United Methodist Church at *www.glide.com.*

• **Put a little *joy* into compliance.** Complying with regulations is rarely seen as a cause for celebration. However, having an efficient, effective, tight control on being in compliance is not an easy task—but it is essential. In large organizations, many people have an influence on the whole. It is not easy to build and maintain an *audit-ready, precision-run* compliance program. It takes constant care, meticulous recordkeeping, seasoned processes that work—and regular, thorough reviews. It is an area where *inspect, don't expect* is the motto to adopt. Taking time to include acknowledgement of successful reviews or enhancements in your compliance program makes several important statements: 1) You recognize the importance of compliance to the organization. 2) You value the hard work it takes. 3) You want more of the same.

• **Count your blessings.** Some of the most significant achievements of your diversity and inclusion efforts may come in the form of *lessons learned.* We don't always think about the sometimes difficult, sometimes joyous, sometimes mundane, sometimes subtle *lessons learned* in the journey to a diverse, inclusive environment as something that should be honored or celebrated. Yet, these *lessons* are the building blocks of knowledge and know-how. Reflecting on *lessons learned* can be a stimulating opportunity for group dialogue, instilling a sense of accomplishment. With a variety of perspectives, you may be surprised at how much has been learned—and that you have reasons to celebrate beyond the numbers. Here are some examples of the kinds of valuable lessons that are often overlooked on our organizational list of accomplishments: 1) Grievances successfully resolved because of new knowledge, new levels of awareness and visible changes in the organization; 2) Recognizing mistakes made due to making wrong assumptions about people; 3) Consciousness raised by getting to know more about the differences in people and learning from them; 4) A grueling audit that ended satisfactorily and provided opportunity to innovate, streamline and document procedures; 5) Discovery of the value of diverse teams working to serve customers, such as opening a new market you were never able to penetrate or reaching new people in the community who you had formally excluded unintentionally.

Results achieved and *lessons learned* springing from our strategies and measures provide excellent opportunities for innovation—and help us gain a sense of accomplishment from many vantage points. Use the MEASURING PROGRESS; CELEBRATING SUCCESS—*Strategies & Measures* exercise on the adjacent page to help you reflect on these ideas, think through your own and formulate plans for action.

MEASURING PROGRESS; CELEBRATING SUCCESS—Strategies & Measures:

Which ideas might be helpful to you?

- ☐ Compare your vision with reality.
- ☐ Celebrate with pictures.
- ☐ Put a little *joy* into compliance.
- ☐ Count your blessings.

For more STRATEGIES & MEASURES strategy ideas see the supporting books and tools in the *Diversity Breakthrough! Strategic Action Series.* To learn more, see page 62.

What ideas do you have for next steps?

____

____

____

____

____

____

What ACTION will you take? ✔ Done

______________________________ Date ________ ☐

______________________________ Date ________ ☐

______________________________ Date ________ ☐

______________________________ Date ________ ☐

______________________________ Date ________ ☐

Add a summary of your plans to your *Diversity & Inclusion Goal-Directed Action Plan* on page 13.

The Power of Potential
... A Story

Sue Swenson
President, Leap Wireless International
CEO, Cricket Communications
Former President & CEO, Cellular One

At the heart of the issues surrounding diversity and inclusion is valuing *substance* instead of just the *form.* It has to be a message that cannot only be heard, but also be visible by your actions. This means always looking for people's potential—what they can bring to the organization—without letting some sort of filter about some test or assessment or some bias get in the way. It means not excluding people from opportunities—taking chances on them that may seem out of the norm.

I've always put a high value on people's experience and expertise—not just their education. I've focused on *what do you bring substantively to a job.* I have recognized that as people develop and grow in the business, they become better leaders, developers and coaches of people, because they have a much better view of what people need—they know what it's like to sit in their chairs and walk in their shoes. It takes awhile for people to see the possibilities. I remember watching people react to promotions. As we promoted some very talented people, who may not have had the opportunity for formal education but contributed significantly to our success, people began to see the possibilities for themselves. Believing in everyone's potential is a living example of *substance over form.* It helps build a new level of credibility, a trust, a feeling of hope and vision of opportunity for employees.

I have found the greatest rewards in staying true to these principles. Seeing what can happen, not only for an individual, but for the rest of the organization, because you did take that chance on someone. It creates a snowball effect, in terms of people seeing opportunity. The energy it releases into the organization is open-ended.

You have to create some consciousness on what your filters and personal biases are. You have to confront them and give people a chance to contribute. You can say all you want about your beliefs in diversity and inclusion, but if you don't take actions to prove it, people won't believe you.

What You Can Do

Staffing & Development

Acknowledging the changing human landscape

Our achievements in creating a diverse, inclusive environment are most visible in the area of staffing and development of our people. You can say all you want about diversity and inclusion, but the human landscape of your organization, how you maintain it and help it grow is proof of your commitment—*the fruits of your labor*—and a message that can be heard without uttering a word. The WHAT YOU CAN DO strategy ideas and suggestions presented in this section are designed to foster your own thinking and actions on how you can:

- profile your achievements in creative ways, and
- radiate success up and down the organization, inside and outside.

Staffing & Development

Acknowledging the changing human landscape

Our accomplishments in staffing and development areas continue to be measured by the human resources *scorecard*—the *numbers.* This is essential to keep us focused on *results achieved,* as well as helping us see when we fall short of the expectations we have established for ourselves. However, Frances Hesselbein, Chairman of the Board of Governors for the *Peter F. Drucker Foundation for Nonprofit Management* raised the bar for all of us, when she started asking the compelling question, *"When they look at us, can they find themselves?"* Suddenly, when considering this question, the numbers have a human face and a human relationship that cannot be hidden in statistics. Noticeably, she left no room for more than a direct response—*yes* or *no.* There is no chance to spin the message more positively when one is faced to admit the truth in the answer—*no.* There is no questioning of a response—no analyzing necessary—if you can answer, *"Yes!"* When you have earned that distinction—or you are well on your way—find ways to acknowledge your success. Here are some ideas of what YOU can do to focus in on your accomplishments and help others do the same:

• **Create a people report card.** Gather data together for your organization. If you are a larger organization you probably have reports that you can refer to with numbers of hires, promotions, training, etc. If you are a small organization, think through what has taken place to recreate the human dynamics of your organization. Since this is a "people report card," get creative and bring your data to *life.* Here is an idea to foster your own creative thinking: 1) Create a newsletter formatted report card, one or two pages. 2) Decide on the staffing and development stories that best represent your achievement (i.e., new hires, new geographic teams, leadership development programs, mentoring and board placements). 3) Find pictures or graphics that will put a human face on these achievement. 4) Integrate brief statistical summaries of results achieved, or use names instead of statistics where possible. 5) Tell brief stories about what has been accomplished. You might add comments from the people profiled to punctuate the achievement. 6) Add a leadership message, honoring accomplishments and creating a *call-to-action* for the continuing journey toward creating a diverse, inclusive environment. 7) Decide on a medium that works for you. At best, it will be one that can be used in a variety of ways. For example, if you format your *People Report Card* as an attractive newsletter-like document, use *Adobe Acrobat, Portable Document File* (PDF)—a cross-platform software, commonly used to create a *print-quality* look and feel. A PDF file can then be loaded on a web, printed for handouts or sent via e-mail—and updated often—all without compromising the style and formatting. Remember, *it is all in how it is presented!* For information on Adobe Acrobat, visit *www.adobe.com.*

- **Expand development experiences.** Part of staffing and development accomplishments is becoming a *learning organization* in every sense of the term. Day-to-day work situations offer many valuable development experiences. Here are some ideas on how to celebrate *learning* by making a focus on what was accomplished part of the *right of passage* to the next level. 1) Talk about every work situation, class, special assignment or team project as a *learning experience.* 2) Make it a practice to point out the not-so-obvious development opportunities within an assignment. 3) Celebrate formal and on-the-job development experiences by having the people present an overview of learnings to others. 4) Include in the requirements of special assignments a *what I learned in the process* presentation to the team. 5) Instill the expectation that continuous learning is the *price-to-stay* for everyone in the organization. 6) Set expectations for senior leaders to set the example by applying the same *rules* to their own development experiences.

- **Cheer mentoring relationships.** Acknowledgements of *mentoring* achievements will do a great deal to inspire new mentoring relationships. Honor the role models of mentoring. Look for those relationships where leaders and subordinates on many levels are exemplifying the *giving and receiving of wisdom.* Bring a few pairs together to share their stories with others on the team. Perhaps it is presented in a way that you acknowledge the mentoring role models by sharing what you have observed about them, followed by a panel discussion with them. Ask the mentoring partners to tell about what they have learned from each other, why the relationship has become important to them and what difference it has made. Then, open up the discussion with questions from your team or audience. It is easier for people to celebrate and follow when they can see the value for themselves.

• **Measure how you've innovated.** Don't just measure the measurable things, look out beyond the data and use it in your message of success. Take time to acknowledge the innovations that have emerged along the way. Look not only at *what* you did in the staffing and development area, but *how* you did it. Here are some things to consider to foster your ideas: 1) New interviewing techniques, procedures and candidate resources that were developed because of your focus; 2) Relationships built with campus and professional organizations, because you had influence, know-how and the people inside the organization to better relate to each group; 3) Diversity awareness achieved through an expanded array of forums, workshops and modules integrated into mainstream development activities; 4) Expanded candidate pool for new board placements that emerged from affiliation with new influential outreach contacts, resulting in your board reflecting the community and marketplace you serve; 5) Retention of top talent due to increased employee satisfaction with the organization's work environment and commitment to diversity and inclusion.

• **Celebrate the growth of individuals.** The strength of future organizations will reside, in part, in their ability to optimize the use of talents and differences in their people. Strength will also mean building a workforce whose members can adapt themselves readily to a wide range of people and situations. Personal attributes are a *must!* Take time to recognize the *strengths* of your people in presenting information, listening to others, relating to a diverse group, getting along with others, respecting others' time, appreciating others' points-of-view, making others comfortable, enjoying others' successes, communicating in writing or in person, demonstrating an interest and willingness to learn from others and adapting oneself to different people and situations. Honor growth. Share your perspectives with the team. Select development activities that will foster more growth.

Diversity and inclusion change the whole experience and human landscape of an organization. Use the MEASURING PROGRESS; CELEBRATING SUCCESS—*Staffing & Development* exercise on the adjacent page to help you reflect on these ideas, think through your own and formulate plans for action.

MEASURING PROGRESS; CELEBRATING SUCCESS—Staffing & Development:

Which ideas might be helpful to you?

- ☐ Create a people report card.
- ☐ Expand development experiences.
- ☐ Cheer mentoring relationships.
- ☐ Measure how you've innovated.
- ☐ Celebrate the growth of individuals.

For more STAFFING & DEVELOPMENT strategy ideas see the supporting books and tools in the *Diversity Breakthrough! Strategic Action Series.* To learn more, see page 62.

What ideas do you have for next steps?

____

____

____

____

____

____

What ACTION will you take? ✔ Done

______________________ Date ________ ☐

______________________ Date ________ ☐

______________________ Date ________ ☐

______________________ Date ________ ☐

______________________ Date ________ ☐

Add a summary of your plans to your *Diversity & Inclusion Goal-Directed Action Plan* on page 13.

Learning to Trust
... A Story

Charles Blodgett
Owner and Landscape Artist
The Burgundy Group

Sometimes the greatest learning comes the second time around. A few years ago, after retiring from IBM, I started a second *career.* My company is located near Atlanta. *The Burgundy Group* specializes in creative, innovative landscaping. After an experience I had working to build houses for the poor in Mexico with my church, I decided that my new business would employ Mexicans that are new to the United States, who were struggling to support families.

Over time, I recognized how valuable this experience has been for me as a person. I have always been a great *talker,* and suddenly I had to learn to listen more and communicate differently with my employees, who spoke only Spanish. Without having all the verbal communication, I find that the outcome is even better. There is a great deal more eye contact between *manager* and *employee*—and a feeling that you are in sync. You have to really pay attention to each other. You learn to convey you are pleased with what they are doing or to read whether they are trying to please you. You find understanding without talking about it. In a short period, a very strong trust is built. Somehow, we soon understand how we benefit each other by what we do. I provide an opportunity and good working conditions. They do excellent work. It doesn't take long to become *simpatico.*

As an IBM manager, there was never an assumed trust on my part. As an employee you had to earn it from me—and because I was the manager, I expected people to come to me. In this business, I have had to trust people because I can't talk about what I want or always be with them with several jobs going at one time. In my entire IBM career, I was incapable of just letting people go—creating a common understanding of our mission and then allowing people to do their best. I always had to be in control—or wanted more control—or thought my ideas were better. Maybe the change has come from a combination of things. I've mellowed. I've learned people work best if given some freedom. Also, my employees have been great teachers. They taught me to trust.

What You Can Do

Ownership

Seeing how far we have come

Being the *owners* of creating an environment that values the differences of all its people and warmly welcomes them into a place to *be* who they are is reflected in our *actions.* Jewish sage, Rabbi Akiva, defined measures of achievements for *ownership* centuries ago, "*...everything is measured according to deeds. Deeds, not feelings. Deeds, not intent. Deeds, not results. Doing itself is good fortune.*" As you find reasons to celebrate your progress in achieving your diversity and inclusion goals, personal ownership and leadership is the most important contribution one can make. Acknowledgement doesn't always mean a standing ovation; it can be quiet—more often acknowledgement coming from a place of gratitude for the *good fortune* of having committed people leading change. The WHAT YOU CAN DO strategy ideas and suggestions presented in this section are designed to foster your own thinking and actions on how you can:

- celebrate diversity making a difference,
- acknowledge personal leadership that led the way, and
- reawaken a sense of purpose and conviction for *more action.*

Ownership

See how far you have come

It takes a great deal of courage to *understand, accept* and *own* the creation of our future workplaces, marketplaces and communities. It is easy to give up when things get tough—to point the finger when the environment is not as welcoming as we had once hoped—when promises have not been kept. However, even in the moments of success, we are also challenged by our own capacity to celebrate our victories and those of others who have shared in the struggle and the joy of progress achieved. Here are some ideas of what YOU can do to focus in on your accomplishments and help others do the same:

• **Be grateful.** Engage your network and support groups, teams and leaders in honoring people who have set an example, helped others, worked tirelessly to implement and present new programs, opened doors, remained tough taskmasters for diversity and inclusion and have truly made a difference in making it everyone's priority. Try to acknowledge people in ways that will be meaningful to them as individuals. You may want to consider a thoughtful letter outlining the specifics of the person's contribution. Perhaps it is a symbolic memento commemorating their important efforts or maybe a personal phone call or visit just to say, *"Thank you."* The more you can be specific about how the person has contributed, the more meaningful your acknowledgement will be. Learning to appreciate others on the *inside* of the organization has a rippling influence when we interact with others *outside.* Gratitude strengthens the goodness that comes from a diverse, inclusive environment. It helps us see how far we have come.

• **Hold an owners' summit.** If you want to have a clear picture of all you have accomplished, honor your key contributors by inviting them to share in a *success summit* designed to identify the answers to two specific questions: *What activities, programs and people have contributed the most to helping you create a diverse, inclusive organization? What specific examples can you share that demonstrate added value to your customers directly or indirectly?*

Create a well-planned agenda that leaves lots of room for dialogue. Listen, listen, listen. Gather the data to broaden your organizational success story—and to be used for refining and opening the way for new contributions. As a finale, ask small groups or pairs to describe what they have learned and what expectations they would like to see fulfilled at a subsequent *summit.* Debrief with the entire group. Use the input to set the stage for celebration and launching next steps.

• **Look outside yourselves to inspire new levels of achievement.** We hear lots about the bad things in our communities and workplaces—somehow we overlook the source of energy and inspiration that comes in the stories of the *ownership* by others. There is so much *good* and so much creativity awaiting our discovery. Do a little research, collecting articles about people making a difference—*taking ownership* for creating a value-based, diverse, inclusive environment. Use a variety of resources, including magazines, the Internet and newsletters, for example. An alternative, have each person on your team find their own example of someone they know or have read about. Reach outside your industry or sector. There is much we can learn from others that will help us figure out how we can contribute more. Save time at a staff meeting or team meeting for sharing these stories. As a framework, explore what the person did, what can be learned from them, how the knowledge could be applied in your organization and what new commitments people are willing to make. Taking time to step inside the life of someone else to explore *ownership* helps us to gain clarity about our own.

• **Believe in people and let them know it every day.** When we work and live in an environment where we feel valued and appreciated, our confidence soars. Honor your people's ownership, first, by knowing each one of them. Develop a keen sense for their qualities and how they fit into your organizational goals and future plans. Solicit their help. Reward it with your acknowledgement when you receive it.

Achievements come from our personal passions in action. Paramahansa Yogananda reminded us when he said, *"A strong will, by its own dynamic force, creates a way for fulfillment of its intention."* Reflecting on how far we have come helps us recognize how powerful personal ownership is in leading change. Use the MEASURING PROGRESS; CELEBRATING SUCCESS —*Ownership* exercise on the next page to help you reflect on these ideas, think through your own and formulate plans for action.

Measuring Progress; Celebrating Success—Ownership:

Which ideas might be helpful to you?

- ☐ Be grateful.
- ☐ Hold an owners' summit.
- ☐ Look outside yourselves to inspire new levels of achievement.
- ☐ Believe in people and let them know it every day.

For more Ownership strategy ideas see the supporting books and tools in the *Diversity Breakthrough! Strategic Action Series.* To learn more, see page 62.

What ideas do you have for next steps?

____

____

____

____

____

____

What action will you take?

		✔ Done
____________________	Date ______	☐
____________________	Date ______	☐
____________________	Date ______	☐
____________________	Date ______	☐
____________________	Date ______	☐

Add a summary of your plans to your *Diversity & Inclusion Goal-Directed Action Plan* on page 13.

A Call to Action

Truth in Numbers

A Message from Debbe Kennedy

They say there is truth in numbers. So, we measure progress for diversity and inclusion on how many of this *sort* and that *type* we have—how many are on the board of directors, how many are in the markets we serve, the community we want to reach, the jobs and levels of stature on the organization chart, in the congregation that fills the pews, the men and women who serve and protect our countries and communities. These are important numbers. They are the benchmarks between our intentions and the results we achieve. They keep us honest to some degree perhaps. Unfortunately, what they don't measure is change in mindset. Change in belief. Change in attitude. Change in heart. Change in the impact of our actions and behaviors on others. Change in our willingness to be inclusive of everyone. The numbers are only signs—easily played with and jockeyed around to make us look good in public mirrors, but do they really tell the truth?

As we march together into a new millennium, we face the challenge of holding ourselves to a higher standard than can be counted in *sorts* and *types.* We have an opportunity to change our vision from the many vantage points we represent, broadening our point of view into a collective purpose. A purpose big enough to result in winning in the marketplace, valuing all people, transforming communities and changing lives. We have more than what we need to do this—will we do it? The opportunity to innovate is here. It comes with raising the bar. The measurement is one of consciousness as individuals, organizations and communities—a change that makes decisions and takes actions ensuring that the implications will serve all people. How do your consciousness and actions measure up? I leave you contemplating this question myself.

"Be the change you wish to see in the world."

—Gandhi

Contributing Organizations

Learning from Role Models

Throughout the world, there is remarkable work being done by many people, organizations and communities to create diverse and inclusive places to live, work and reach our potential as individuals. It is a movement spreading across all industries and sectors—and role models are emerging to help lead the way in creating the workplaces and communities of the 21st Century.

A common feature of the *Diversity Breakthrough! Strategic Action Series* is bringing real stories from people leading change in their organizations. The special stories woven into the messages in this *Achievement: Measuring Progress; Celebrating Success* book were generously shared during a personal interview with these exemplary leaders. Collectively, this group of distinguished change leaders and their organizations represent a sampling of the *difference makers* working to lead the way for transformation of our workplaces, businesses—big and small, nonprofit organizations, schools, government, military and our communities—transforming them into places that embrace change, value diversity and include everybody. It is with deep gratitude and admiration that each is introduced and honored here:

Lowell Area Schools, *Foreword* by:
Bert Bleke, Superintendent

Selected for their approach of involving the whole community one important step at a time. Learn more: *www.lowell.k12.mi.us*

CDV - Clients Deserve Value, *Smiles Are Passports* story by:
Catherine DeVrye
Author, *Good Service Is Good Business, Japan: An A to Z* and *The Customer Service Zoo*
1993 Australian Executive Woman of the Year

Selected for her living example of leadership. She speaks to organizations around the world on managing change, customer service and turning obstacles into opportunities from a cross-cultural perspective. Learn more: *www.ozemail.com.au/~cdv*

IBM Corporation, *Bringing People Together* story by:
J. T. (Ted) Childs, Jr., Vice President, Global Workforce Diversity

Selected for their heritage of leadership for diversity and inclusion around the world. Learn more: *www.ibm.com*

Hewlett-Packard Company, *New Language for Success* story by:
Emily Duncan, Director, Global Diversity & Work/Life

Selected for setting an example of worldwide management leadership and the deeply held beliefs and practices of the HP Way that value people. Learn more: *www.hp.com*

United States Army, *Achievement Without Numbers* story by:
David H. Ohle
Lieutenant General, U.S. Army
Deputy Chief of Staff for Personnel

Selected for their forward-thinking, systemized approach to change that is the force behind their work to create a flexible, focused, diverse and inclusive organization for the 21st Century. Learn more: *www.army.mil*

Leap Wireless International, *The Power of Potential* story by:
Sue Swenson, President, Leap Wireless International and CEO, Cricket Communications. Former President & CEO, Cellular One

Selected for the leadership example of environment, processes and business practices that integrate fundamental fairness, diversity and inclusion into mainstream day-to-day operations. Learn more: *www.leapwireless.com*

The Burgundy Group, Inc., *Learning to Trust* story by:
Charles Blodgett, Owner and Landscape Artist
Former Northwestern Area Manager of IBM Management Development.

Selected for setting an example of leadership, growth and renewal.

Notes and Sources

The following books and other resources listed have provided information, fostered ideas and have been a continuous source of inspiration for this work. I am grateful to these messengers.

Barker, Joel A., *Wealth, Innovation & Diversity* video, and *Paradigm Pioneers video,* Starthrower Distribution, *www.starthrower.com,* 800-242-3220.

Benson, Roland, "Cultural Diversity in Health Care is Part of Good Customer Service," South Florida Business Journal, Broward Edition, July 7, 1997, *www.amcity.com.*

Carr-Ruffino, Norma, *Diversity Success Strategies,* Butterworth-Heinemann, 1999.

Cox, Jr., Taylor and Beale, Ruby L., *Developing Competency to Manage Diversity: Readings, Cases & Activities,* Berrett-Koehler Publishers, 1997 and *Cultural Diversity in Organizations: Theory, Research & Practice,* Berrett-Koehler Publishers, 1994.

Diversity/Careers in Engineering & Information Technology, "Diversity In Action: Short Profiles of Diversity Activities at Specific Companies, www.diversitycareers.com

Ellinor, Linda and Gerard, Glenna, *Dialogue: Rediscover the Transforming Power of Conversation,* John Wiley & Sons, 1998

FORTUNE, *"Where Diversity Really Works,"* July 19, 1999, *www.fortune.com.*

Hesselbein, Frances, "When They Look at Us, Can They Find Themselves" by Frances Hesselbein, Editor-In-Chief, *Leader to Leader,* A Publication of the Drucker Foundation and Jossey-Bass Publishers, Number 1, Winter 1999

Huang, Chungliang Al and Jerry Lynch, *Mentoring: The Tao of Giving and Receiving Wisdom,* HarperSanFrancisco, 1995.

Inamori, Kazuo, *Passion for Success: Practical, Inspirational, and Spiritual Insight from Japan's Leading Entrepreneur,* McGraw-Hill, Inc. 1995

Barbara "BJ" Hateley and Warren H. Schmidt, *A Peacock in the Land of Penguins: A Tale of Diversity and Discovery,* Berrett-Koehler Publishers, 1995, 1997.

Pfeffer, Jeffrey and John F. Veiga, "Putting People First for Organizational Success," *The Academy of Management Executive,* Volume 13, Number 2, May 1999, Page 37-48.

Shaffer, Carolyn R. and Anundsen, Kristen, *Creating Community Anywhere: Finding Support and Connection in a Fragmented World,* Jeremy P. Tarcher/Putnam, 1993

Shapiro, Rabbi Rami M., *Wisdom of the Jewish Sages: A Modern Reading of Pirke Avot,* Bell Tower, 1993.

Speak to My Heart: Communities of Faith and Contemporary African American Life, Smithsonian Anacostia Museum, May 1999.

Thomas, R. Roosevelt, Jr., *Redefining Diversity,* American Management Association, 1996

Turner, Maelinda, President of the Class of 1991, Oberlin College, *"Vernon Johns: Farmer, Preacher, Civil-rights Pioneer," www.oberlin.edu.*

The Diversity Factor, Fall 1998, Volume 7, Number 1, Published by Elsie Y. Cross Associates, P.O. Bos 3188, Teaneck, NJ 07666.

About the Author

Debbe Kennedy is a writer, problem-solver and facilitator. She is also founder and president of the Leadership Solutions Companies, specializing in leadership and organizational communications. She is the author of *Breakthrough!: Everything You Need to Start a Solution Revolution,* which received the 1998 InnoThink Award "for the most far-reaching combination of message and media," given by MANAGEMENT GENERAL®.

Kennedy, a former manager of Equal Opportunity for IBM Corporation, has had a long-held conviction and continuing leadership influence in working to help organizations work toward achieving the ideals of a diverse, inclusive environment. Her efforts have resulted in award-winning corporate leadership communications solutions and training products distributed throughout the world. She knows the leader's journey as you do. Kennedy has walked it as a successful entrepreneur, a change-leading strategic partner for Fortune 100 executives, managers and community leaders and in a rewarding leadership career with IBM Corporation that included 15 years as a manager of people and human resource programs. She was recognized three consecutive years by IBM Management Development for her contributions and innovations in the area of leadership and human resource development.

For ongoing support and information visit:
www.diversitybreakthrough.com

To learn more about Debbe Kennedy's work and other *Breakthrough!* products, visit www.lscompanies.com. You can contact Debbe Kennedy at dkennedy@lscompanies.com.

About the Diversity Breakthrough! Strategic Action Series
by Debbe Kennedy

The *Diversity Breakthrough! Strategic Action Series* was created to support leaders and organizations (businesses, workplaces or communities) that are working to create productive and welcoming inclusive environments that value the diversity and talent of all people. The series includes the *Diversity Breakthrough! Action Dialogues* and *eight* other supporting action-directed books and tools. Each of the nine *Diversity Breakthrough!* products is designed to bring stand-alone value, independent of the others. They are also designed to work together as a system. This makes it possible for *any* or *all* of the components in the series to be used together in any combination that meets your changing needs and priorities.

The entire series is built on the premise that creating a diverse and inclusive organization, business, workplace or community requires a *perpetual cycle of action* (Figure 1, page 10). A description of each *action-directed* product in the series follows.

Description of the *Diversity Breakthrough! Strategic Action Series* Products:

Action Dialogues: Meaningful Conversations to Accelerate Change ISBN 1-58376-056-3 Item No. 60563 A complete set of tools to conduct three distinctive *action dialogues.* It comes with an *Action Dialogues* book and illustrated cards to facilitate conversations around the often sensitive and tough issues associated with creating a diverse and inclusive environment. Issue themes include: leadership, culture, involvement, business, strategies and measures, staffing and development, and ownership. The dialogue framework guides you through an exploration of what is working, what is standing in the way and next steps for action. Designed for your own personal exploration and self-assessments, one-on-one conversations or small group dialogues. Boxed for travel.

Assessment: Defining Current Realities ISBN 1-58376-050-4 Item No. 60504 How to take an in-depth look at your organization to determine the *current realities* and *inhibitors* related to creating a *diverse, inclusive* environment. Action strategies, stories, insights and ideas for *what* and *how* to do ASSESSMENTS in *seven* key areas that influence organizational effectiveness.

Acceptance: Developing Support for Change ISBN 1-58376-051-2 Item No. 60512 How to develop support for change in your organization, including leadership, sponsorship, manager conviction and buy-in from everyone involved. Action strategies, stories, insights and ideas for *what* and *how* to gain ACCEPTANCE of the need for change and understanding of its implications in *seven* key areas that influence organizational effectiveness.

Action: Moving Forward ISBN 1-58376-052-0 Item No. 60520 How to *launch* a new diversity and inclusion initiative or *revitalize* and *renew* an existing initiative in your organization (business, workplace or community). Action strategies, stories, insights and ideas for *what* and *how* to take ACTION in *seven* key areas that influence organizational effectiveness.

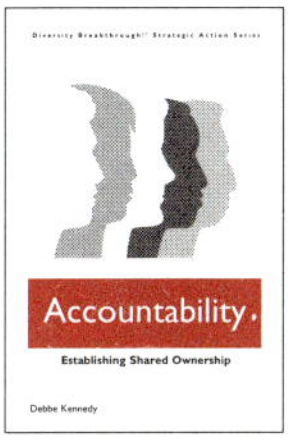

Accountability: Establishing Shared Ownership ISBN 1-58376-053-9 Item No. 60539 How to develop shared ownership and accountability with consideration of *seven* key areas of influence. Action strategies, stories, insights and ideas for *how* to establish shared ACCOUNTABILITY for diversity and inclusion, including integrating it into mainstream principles, strategies, scorecard, individual contribution and with considerations in each of *seven* key areas that influence organizational effectiveness.

Achievement: Measuring Progress; Celebrating Success ISBN 1-58376-054-7 Item No. 60547 How to monitor, measure and celebrate progress as you work to create a diverse, inclusive organization. Action strategies, stories, insights and ideas for *what* and *how* to monitor, measure and celebrate ACHIEVEMENT and progress with consideration to *seven* key areas that influence organizational effectiveness.

More Action: Keeping Momentum Alive! ISBN 1-58376-055-5 Item No. 60555 How to re-evaluate, renew commitment and start a next phase of ACTION in your organization. Action strategies, stories, insights and ideas for *what* and *how* to keep momentum *alive* with MORE ACTION with consideration of *seven* key areas that influence organizational effectiveness.

FORTHCOMING PRODUCTS IN THE SERIES

Diversity & Inclusion: Action-Prompters and Leadership Insights to Accelerate Change. A book of 52 personalized action-prompters for change leaders. Each page is illustrated and includes a thought-provoking insight from a notable *change leader.* Follows the same thought-provoking, action-prompting themes used throughout the *Diversity Breakthrough! Strategic Action Series.* A meaningful gift, meeting memento or tool for your own desk or diversity and inclusion tool kit.

Diversity Breakthrough! Action Dialogues for Teams: A Multiple Group Conversation Includes a comprehensive step-by-step *action dialogue leader's* facilitation guide for holding a session with multiple small work teams (4 teams, 4–6 per team). Uses the *Diversity Breakthrough! Action Dialogue* concepts, processes and tools. Comes with five *Diversity Breakthrough! Action Dialogues* illustrated card decks. Great for dialogues with teams, a diversity training session, community forum, management development activity or leadership meeting workshop.

Berrett-Koehler Communications • P.O. Box 565 • Williston • VT 05495-9900
800-929-2929 • Fax: 802-864-7626 • www.bkconnection.com

About Berrett-Koehler Communications

Berrett-Koehler Communications was created to support the movement toward a more enlightened world of work and more free, open, humane, effective and globally sustainable organizations. Our publishing agenda covers the following areas:

- Leadership, Management, Stewardship
- Work and Careers, Personal Development
- Organizational Change and Development
- Human Resource Management and Development
- Business and Global Sustainability

We seek new projects on leading-edge topics that will provide business and allied audiences with practical guidance, new thinking or critical analysis and advocacy in brief, easily digestible packets. Berrett-Koehler Communications' publications will be designed to stimulate thought and discussion; we encourage controversy and a diversity of voices.

To learn more, visit www.bkconnection.com.